ITALIAN FINGER FOOD

BY NICOLE HERFT

CONTENTS

INTRODUCTION

There's a saying in Italy, 'La cucina è il cuore della casa' which translates to 'The kitchen is the heart of the home'. For Italians, food is what brings family and friends together, which is such a wonderful yet simple sentiment.

My very first job was at an Italian restaurant in Australia, which inspired me to train as a chef, and I've been passionate about Italian food ever since. Italy is by far my favourite holiday destination too – great food, wine, people, history, hospitality and culture. What more could you want? Tuscany, Sardinia, Milan, Cinque Terre and Positano are just a few of my all-time favourites, and I never tire of visiting them.

These days I work as a food stylist and am no longer a chef in a restaurant. Being a food stylist has taught me how important it is for food to initially grab you by the way it looks. I hope you agree that the dishes in Little Italy *are visually beautiful, and taste 'deliziosa'. I wanted to share my recipes with you so you too can impress your friends and family with your cooking prowess.*

All the recipes in this book are simple and flavourful. Italian finger food is designed around entertaining so I hope you have as much fun making them for your friends as I did making them especially for you.

'Mangia bene, ridi spesso, ama molto' – *Eat well, laugh often, love much.*

Buon appetito!

Nicole Herft

PUMPKIN, SAGE <u>AND</u> TALEGGIO ARANCINI

These gorgeous rice balls originate from Sicily. Pumpkin and sage are one of my favourite taste combinations and work so well together here. Along with the melted burst of Taleggio tucked inside each one, of course.

› 2 tablespoons olive oil

› 250 g (9 oz/1⅔ cups) pumpkin or butternut squash, finely chopped

› sea salt and freshly ground black pepper

› 1½ tablespoons unsalted butter

› 1 onion, finely chopped

› 2 garlic cloves, finely chopped

› 250 g (9 oz/1⅔ cups) arborio rice

› 1 litre (34 fl oz) hot chicken stock

› 40 g (1½ oz/½ cup) grated Parmesan

› 2 tablespoons sage leaves, plus extra to serve

› 200 g (7 oz) Taleggio

› vegetable oil to deep-fry

› 1 quantity tomato sauce (page 14), to serve

COATING

› 150 g (5 oz/1¼ cups) plain (all-purpose) flour

› 2 large eggs, lightly beaten

› 250 g (9 oz/2½ cups) white breadcrumbs

Heat half of the olive oil in a non-stick frying pan over a high heat. Add the pumpkin, season with salt and pepper and cook for 10 minutes.

Heat the remaining oil and the butter in a large saucepan, add the onion and cook until softened. Add the garlic and cook for 2 minutes, then tip in the rice and stir well to coat each grain. Increase the heat and add a ladle of stock, stirring until all the liquid is absorbed. Repeat until all the stock has been used and the rice is creamy and cooked al dente. Remove from the heat and stir through the pumpkin, parmesan and sage. Season to taste and allow the mixture to cool. Cover and refrigerate to chill.

When the mixture has cooled, divide it into 30 balls and flatten. Cut the Taleggio into 1 cm (½ in) cubes and place it in the centre of the flattened ball, then mould the rice around it to form a round ball again. Put the flour, eggs and breadcrumbs in separate bowls. Roll each ball in flour, dip in egg, then coat in breadcrumbs.

Heat up the vegetable oil to 180°C (350°F). Deep fry the arancini in batches for 4–5 minutes or until golden brown. Drain on paper towels. Take a handful of sage leaves and fry them in the hot oil for around 30 seconds. Take care as you do so, because they will splatter. Remove them from the oil and drain well. Sprinkle the arancini with sea salt and the deep-fried sage leaves. Serve with the tomato sauce for dipping.

FENNEL, SALAMI <u>AND</u> GOAT'S CHEESE BRUSCHETTE

Finocchiona is a very popular Tuscan pork salami, flavoured with fennel seeds and herbs. It's perfect here with slices of fennel and smooth, creamy goat's cheese. It tastes great with artichokes, too.

› 12 slices of ciabatta

› 3 tablespoons extra-virgin olive oil

› 1 garlic clove

› 3 baby fennel bulbs

› 200 g (7 oz) soft goat's cheese

› 1–2 tablespoons milk

› sea salt and freshly ground black pepper

› 24 slices fennel salami (finocchiona)

› 2 teaspoons fennel seeds, lightly toasted

› few sprigs of dill

› extra-virgin olive oil, to serve

Brush each side of the ciabatta slices with olive oil and place on a hot griddle pan over a high heat until charred marks appear, turning to char both sides. Remove from the pan and rub each piece with the garlic clove.

Using a mandolin or a very sharp knife, trim and thinly slice each bulb of fennel into long strips.

Break up the goat's cheese into a medium bowl, add the milk and some seasoning and whisk until smooth. Thickly spread the mixture over each slice of ciabatta. Top each with a couple of slices of salami and fennel. Sprinkle with the fennel seeds and dill sprigs, drizzle with a little extra-virgin olive oil and serve with a cold glass of Prosecco.

SALAMI, ROAST PEPPER <u>AND</u> SCAMORZA PIZZETTES

Feel free to use your favourite type of salami in this recipe. The sweetness of the roasted peppers paired with the spicy salami and smoky scamorza makes this irresistible. You won't be able to stop at one, I assure you.

DOUGH
› **500 g (1 lb 2 oz/4 cups) '00' flour, plus extra to dust**
› **100 g (3½ oz/⅗ cup) fine semolina**
› **½ teaspoon fine sea salt**
› **7 g (¼ oz) sachet fast-action yeast**
› **1 teaspoon golden caster sugar (unrefined superfine sugar)**
› **3 tablespoons extra-virgin olive, plus more to oil**

TOMATO SAUCE
› **2 tablespoons olive oil**
› **1 shallot, finely chopped**
› **1 garlic clove, crushed**
› **400 g (14 oz) can chopped plum tomatoes**
› **1 tablespoon tomato purée (paste)**
› **½ teaspoon dried oregano**
› **sea salt and freshly ground black pepper**

TOPPINGS
› **2 roasted red (bell) peppers**
› **200 g (7 oz) scamorza**
› **24 slices Napoli salami, torn**

Begin by making the dough. Sift both flours into a large bowl, add the salt and mix well. In a separate bowl, mix the yeast, sugar, oil and 325 ml (11 fl oz) of lukewarm water. Leave to activate for a few minutes. Make a well in the centre of the flour and add the mixture; stir well until it forms a dough. Remove the dough from the bowl and place on a lightly floured work surface. Knead until smooth and elastic, for 4–5 minutes. Place the dough into a clean bowl and cover with a lightly oiled piece of plastic wrap. Leave in a warm place until the dough doubles in size; this should take around 30 minutes, depending on how warm your chosen spot is.

Meanwhile, to make the sauce, heat the olive oil in a saucepan, add the shallot and cook until translucent. Add the garlic, tomatoes, purée, oregano, salt and pepper and cook for a further 10 minutes. Blend the sauce until smooth.

Preheat the oven to 200°C (400°F/Gas 6). Dust the work surface with flour and roll out the dough to 3 mm (¼ in) thick. Using an 8 cm (3¼ in) round pastry cutter, cut out 24 rounds of dough and lay them on 2 baking trays lined with baking paper.

Finely slice the red pepper and scamorza. Spread a teaspoon of sauce on each round, evenly scatter over the toppings and season. Bake for 10 minutes. Remove from the oven and serve.

GARLIC, PRAWN AND ROCKET PIZZETTES

For those of you that have never tried seafood on a pizza before... get involved!

› **1 quantity dough (page 14)**
› **1 quantity tomato sauce (page 14)**

TOPPINGS

› **24 tiger prawns (jumbo shrimp)**
› **2 tablespoons extra-virgin olive oil**
› **3 garlic cloves, finely sliced**
› **1½ long red chillies, finely sliced**
› **1 small fennel bulb**
› **sea salt and freshly ground black pepper**
› **grated zest of 1 lemon**
› **25 g (1 oz/1 cup) rocket (arugula) leaves**

Make the dough and sauce as on page 14.

Preheat the oven to 200°C (400°F/Gas 6). Form 24 pizzettes, as on page 14.

Mix the prawns, oil, garlic, chilli and fennel together in a bowl and season well.

Spread a teaspoon of sauce on each round of dough. Divide the prawn mixture over the rounds and bake in the oven for 10 minutes.

Sprinkle over the lemon zest and top each with a few rocket leaves. Serve immediately.

Top left: Garlic, Prawn and Rocket Pizzette. Centre: Salami, Roast Pepper and Scamorza Pizzette. Bottom left: Vegetarian Pizzette.

VEGETARIAN PIZZETTES

Pizza is Italy's most famous dish and these mini versions are perfect for simple entertaining. They can be made in advance and left in the refrigerator until your guests arrive. Pop them in the oven for ten minutes and they're ready.

› **1 quantity dough (page 14)**
› **1 quantity tomato sauce (page 14)**

TOPPINGS

› **2 baby courgettes (zucchini), sliced**
› **100 g (3½ oz/¾ cup) pitted olives, halved**
› **8 button mushrooms, sliced**
› **8 yellow and/or red cherry tomatoes, halved**
› **1–2 balls of mozzarella**
› **small basil leaves, to garnish**

Make the dough and sauce as on page 14.

Preheat the oven to 200°C (400°F/Gas 6). Form 24 pizzettes, as on page 14.

Spread 1 teaspoon of sauce on each round. Arrange the courgettes, olives, mushrooms and cherry tomatoes on top of each one. Slice the mozzerella and divide between the rounds. Bake for 10 minutes.

Remove from the oven, top with a few basil leaves and serve.

SCALLOPS <u>WITH</u> CRISPY PANCETTA <u>AND</u> GREMOLATA

A scallop is a thing of beauty, so sweet and delicate. It should never be ruined by cooking it with too many other flavours. Keep it simple. As a starter, this delightlful dish will serve six.

› 12 large scallops, roes removed

› 1 garlic clove, finely chopped

› sea salt and freshly ground black pepper

› 3 tablespoons olive oil

› 150 g (5 oz/1 cup) pancetta, finely chopped

› a knob of butter

GREMOLATA

› small bunch of flat-leaf parsley, finely chopped

› finely grated zest of 1 lemon

› 1 small garlic clove, finely chopped

Marinate the scallops: mix them in a bowl with the garlic, some seasoning and 1 tablespoon of olive oil. Cover and leave for 20 minutes.

Add the pancetta to a hot non-stick frying pan and cook for around 5 minutes or until golden and crispy all over. Remove the pancetta with a slotted spoon and transfer to a plate lined with paper towels to drain.

Mix the gremolata ingredients together.

Wipe out the pan, place over a high heat and add another tablespoon of olive oil. Add half of the scallops to the pan and cook for 20 seconds on one side. Flip them over and add half the butter. Cook for another 20 seconds, then remove from the pan. Keep warm while you repeat with the remaining oil, scallops and butter.

Serve them up in small scallop shells or spoons, each sprinkled with pancetta and a little gremolata.

MINI CAPRESE SALADS

Use both yellow and red cherry tomatoes in this dish to make it as colourful as possible. It's another Italian classic of simple flavours that work brilliantly together. Alternatively you could also enjoy this as a light lunch.

› **350 g (12 oz/2½ cups) cherry or baby plum tomatoes, mixed colours if possible**
› **250 g (9 oz/2 cups) baby bocconcini balls (mini mozzarella balls)**
› **handful of baby basil leaves**
› **sea salt and freshly ground black pepper**
› **4 tablespoons balsamic vinegar**
› **6 tablespoons extra-virgin olive oil**

Slice the cherry tomatoes and put them in a large bowl. Add the bocconcini, basil and salt and pepper.

Spoon this mixture into 10 serving glasses. Mix the balsamic and olive oil together and season to taste. Pour a little over each Caprese salad and serve the remaining alongside, either in a jug with a spout or in a dish with a spoon, so your guests can add more if they fancy it.

CRAB-STUFFED BABY ARTICHOKES

Get your hands on the freshest white crab meat and make this dish in less than ten minutes. It doesn't get any simpler.

› **250 g (9 oz/2 cups) fresh white crab meat**
› **juice and finely grated zest of 1 lemon**
› **1 red chilli, deseeded and finely chopped**
› **½ fennel bulb, finely chopped**
› **4 tablespoons extra-virgin olive oil**
› **2 tablespoons flat-leaf parsley leaves, finely chopped**
› **sea salt and freshly ground black pepper**
› **9 pre-cooked and marinated baby artichokes with stems, halved lengthwise**
› **lemon wedges, to serve**

In a bowl, mix the crab meat, lemon juice and zest, chilli, fennel, olive oil and half the parsley. Season to taste with salt and pepper.

Prep the artichokes by scooping out a little from the centre of each heart using a melon baller or a teaspoon. Lay the halved artichokes on a platter and spoon the crab mixture into the hollow you created. Sprinkle with the remaining parsley and serve with lemon wedges.

PORK <u>AND</u> FENNEL POLPETTE

Pork and fennel have been best friends for a very long time. They go so well together and this dish showcases what's so perfect about their friendship. The toasted fennel seeds and fennel bulb in the sauce are just superb.

› 500 g (1 lb 2 oz/2¼ cups) minced (ground) pork
› 2 garlic cloves, crushed
› 1 tablespoon fennel seeds, lightly toasted and ground
› pinch of chilli flakes
› 1 egg, lightly beaten
› 50 g (2 oz/½ cup) fresh breadcrumbs
› sea salt and freshly ground black pepper
› 2 tablespoons olive oil

TOMATO AND FENNEL SAUCE

› 2 tablespoons olive oil
› 1 small fennel bulb, finely chopped, plus fennel fronds, to garnish
› 150 ml (5 fl oz) white wine
› 400 g (14 oz) can chopped tomatoes
› 200 ml (7 fl oz) tomato passata (puréed tomatoes)
› dill sprigs, to garnish

Put the pork, garlic, fennel seeds, chilli, egg, breadcrumbs and seasoning into a large bowl and massage the meat with your hands until well combined.

Take small amounts of the mixture and roll into 24 walnut-sized balls or log shapes. Cover and refrigerate for 1 hour to firm up.

Next, heat the olive oil in a large non-stick frying pan over a medium-high heat and cook the polpette in two batches until lightly browned all over. Transfer to a plate.

Now make the sauce: add the olive oil to the pan and gently sauté the fennel until soft. Deglaze the pan with the wine and allow it to reduce by half before adding the tomatoes and passata. Allow to cook gently for 10 minutes. Return the polpette to the pan and cook for a further 5 minutes or until cooked through.

Spoon the polpette on to individual serving dishes and garnish with fennel fronds and dill sprigs.

TRUFFLED FIGS WITH BRESAOLA AND ROCKET

Sometimes the simple things are often the best... Once you've tried this recipe, it will be something you will make again and again. If you've never tasted truffled honey before, prepare to become addicted!

> 5 small figs, quartered

> 2 tablespoons truffled honey

> 2 tablespoons balsamic vinegar

> 2 tablespoons extra-virgin olive oil

> 40 thin bresaola (Italian cured beef) slices

> 50 g (2 oz/2 cups) rocket (arugula) leaves

Place the figs, honey, balsamic and olive oil into a bowl and allow the flavours to combine. When you are ready to serve, remove the figs from the dressing and set aside on a plate.

Arrange 2 slices of bresaola around each piece of fig, tucking a few sprigs of rocket inside. This can be a little slippery so the best way to do it is: lay the bresaola down first, place the fig and rocket in the middle and tightly wrap the meat around, folding it down to expose the figs. Sit them upright and mould them on the plate gently.

Drizzle with any extra dressing that is left in the bowl.

CURED MEAT CROSTINI

I absolutely adore Italian cured meats and have picked three of my favourites for these crostini, though you can put whatever you like on these to make the recipe your own. Feel free to use basil pesto or sundried tomato pesto instead of tapenade, if you like.

› **20 x 1 cm (½ in)-thick slices of ciabatta**
› **extra-virgin olive oil**
› **150 g (5 oz/½ cup) tapenade**
› **5 slices of mortadella, each cut into quarters**
› **10 slices of prosciutto, halved**
› **20 thin slices of salami**
› **10 cherry tomatoes, halved**
› **20 large caper berries**

Brush the ciabatta with olive oil on both sides and place on a hot griddle for around 30 seconds on each side until light charred marks appear.

Spread each crostini with tapenade.

Arrange a piece each of mortadella, prosciutto and salami on each crostini. Add a half cherry tomato and a caper berry to each, then serve.

MINI FRITTO MISTO CONES <u>WITH</u> SALSA VERDE

Instant happiness with just two words: 'Fritto Misto'. Golden, crispy morsels of your favourite seafood. Make sure your oil is hot enough and you won't go wrong. These light and crispy treats work perfectly with salsa verde.

› **1.75 kg (3 lb 14 oz) mixture of seafood, such as baby squid, prawn (shrimp), whitebait (fish fry), firm white fish fillets, salmon fillets and scallops**
› **vegetable oil, to deep-fry**
› **190 g (6⅔ oz/1½ cups) plain (all-purpose) flour**
› **sea salt**
› **3 tablespoons olive oil**
› **350 ml (11 fl oz) sparkling water**
› **1 egg white**
› **lemon wedges, to serve**

SALSA VERDE
› **4 tablespoons flat-leaf parsley leaves, finely chopped**
› **2 tablespoons mint leaves, finely chopped**
› **4 tablespoons extra-virgin olive oil**
› **2 small garlic cloves, finely chopped**
› **1 tablespoon capers, chopped**
› **3 anchovy fillets, finely chopped**
› **1 tablespoon red wine vinegar**
› **1 teaspoon Dijon mustard**

Begin by mixing all the ingredients together for the salsa verde, season well and taste. Add a little more vinegar if need be or a little more oil to loosen. Set aside until needed.

Prepare the seafood: clean and trim tentacles from the squid, shell and devein the prawns leaving the tails on, remove roes from the scallops, and then cut everything (except the prawns) into similar-sized pieces so they cook evenly. Place in a bowl and season well.

Heat the oil until it measures 190°C (375°F) on an oil thermometer. (If you don't have one of those, a cube of bread thrown in should turn golden brown in 20 seconds.)

Meanwhile, sift the flour into a large bowl, add a big pinch of salt and whisk in the olive oil. Continue whisking and slowly add the sparkling water until well combined. In a separate bowl, whisk the egg white until stiff peaks form, then gently fold into the batter.

Take handfuls of the seafood, coat lightly in the batter and fry in the hot oil in batches for 1–2 minutes or until cooked through and golden brown. Drain on paper towels and keep warm while you cook the rest. Sprinkle with salt and serve in mini newspaper cones with the salsa verde and lemon wedges on the side.

CRAB, COURGETTE, CHILLI <u>AND</u> LEMON LINGUINE POTS

Classic flavours that work so well together. I love to use both brown and white crab meat because they each offer something very different. The crème fraîche and lemon give this a lovely light finish.

› **extra-virgin olive oil**
› **2 garlic cloves, finely chopped**
› **1 red chilli, deseeded and finely chopped**
› **1 courgette (zucchini), cut into very fine strips**
› **200 g (7 oz/1½ cups) white crab meat**
› **50 g (2 oz/⅓ cup) brown crab meat**
› **300 g (10½ oz) fresh linguine**
› **3 tablespoons crème fraîche**
› **sea salt and freshly ground black pepper**
› **finely grated zest and juice of 1 lime**
› **leaves from a small bunch of flat-leaf parsley**
› **25 g (1 oz/1 cup) watercress, to garnish**

Heat the oil in a sauté pan over a gentle heat and cook the garlic and chilli for a couple of minutes. Add the courgette and cook for 2 minutes, stir in the crab meat until just warmed through, then remove from the heat.

Meanwhile, cook the linguine in boiling salted water until al dente, drain and transfer to a bowl.

Add half the crab mixture to the pasta with the crème fraîche, seasoning and lime juice. Mix well and divide between 12 mini serving bowls or mini pots, twirling the pasta around serving forks. Gently reheat the remaining crab mixture, remove it from the heat and stir through the parsley.

Top each bowl of linguine with a little crab mixture, sprinkle with lime zest and garnish with a sprig of watercress.

MINESTRONE SOUP CUPS

This is a healthy and hearty soup, packed with flavour. You can add whatever vegetables are in season; almost anything will work.

› 2 tablespoons olive oil
› 1 small onion, finely chopped
› 1 small carrot, finely chopped
› ½ fennel bulb, core removed, finely chopped
› 2 celery stalks, finely chopped
› 2 garlic cloves, crushed
› 2 sprigs of rosemary, leaves picked and finely chopped
› 1.2 litres (2 pints) vegetable stock
› 100 g (3½ oz/⅔ cup) dried tiny soup pasta shapes
› 200 g (7 oz/1 cup) canned borlotti beans, drained and rinsed
› 2 plum tomatoes, deseeded and finely chopped
› 2 handfuls cavolo nero (Italian black kale) or swiss chard (silverbeet), chopped
› extra-virgin olive oil
› grated Parmesan, to serve
› baby basil leaves, to serve
› toasted ciabatta, to serve

Heat the olive oil in a large saucepan over a low heat and add the onion, carrot, fennel, celery, garlic and rosemary. Cook, stirring now and then, for 10 minutes or until the vegetables have softened.

Pour in the stock, increase the heat and bring to a simmer. Add the pasta, beans, tomatoes and cavolo nero and cook for a further 8 minutes or until the pasta is cooked.

Spoon into small cups to serve. Drizzle with extra-virgin olive oil, sprinkle with a little Parmesan and baby basil leaves. Serve with hot slices of ciabatta.

SPAGHETTI BOLOGNESE MINI BOWLS

This version is so quick, but you still end up with a deliciously rich sauce.
The mini bowls in the picture are perfect for cocktail parties.

› 2 tablespoons olive oil
› 50 g (2 oz/⅓ cup) pancetta, finely chopped
› ½ onion, finely chopped
› 1 garlic clove, crushed
› 2 sprigs of rosemary, leaves picked and finely chopped
› 300 g (10½ oz/1¼ cups) minced (ground) beef
› 150 ml (5 fl oz) red wine
› 2 tablespoons sundried tomato purée (paste)
› 1 ½ x 400 g (14 oz) cans chopped tomatoes (600 g/1 lb 5 oz)
› 150 ml (5 fl oz) beef stock
› sea salt and freshly ground black pepper
› 200 g (7 oz) spaghetti
› Parmesan shavings, to serve

Place a saucepan over a medium heat, add the oil and pancetta and cook for a couple of minutes. Add the onion, garlic and rosemary and cook until the onions have softened. Crumble in the beef and break it up well with a wooden spoon until it begins to brown. Pour in the wine and allow it to reduce by half. Add the purée, tomatoes and stock, reduce the heat to a gentle simmer and allow the sauce to cook for 20 minutes. Taste and season well.

Cook the spaghetti until al dente and drain. Mix half the sauce with the spaghetti; twirl the spaghetti bolognese around serving forks and place in little cups or inside tiny bowls. Top each with a spoon more sauce and sprinkle with Parmesan shavings.

COURGETTE FRITTI WITH SMOKED GARLIC AÏOLI

What's not to love here? Golden, crispy courgette fries served with a creamy, smoky, garlicky aïoli. This is one of my all-time favourites. They never last long.

› **2 large courgettes (zucchini)**
› **200 g (7 oz/1½ cups) '00' flour**
› **100 ml (3½ fl oz) olive oil**
› **2 egg whites**
› **vegetable oil, to shallow-fry**

SMOKED GARLIC AÏOLI

› **3 small smoked garlic cloves, crushed**
› **¼ teaspoon smoked paprika, or to taste**
› **2 egg yolks**
› **juice of 1 lemon**
› **sea salt and freshly ground black pepper**
› **100 ml (3½ fl oz) mild-flavoured olive oil**

Prepare the the courgette by slicing it on an angle, ½ cm (¼ in) thick. Lay down these slices and cut into thick matchsticks.

Make a batter: put the flour in a large bowl, make a well in the centre and whisk in the oil and a tablespoon of warm water. Gradually add more water if necessary to create a batter that's the consistency of double cream. Place the egg whites into a clean bowl.

Start on the aïoli: put the garlic, paprika, egg yolks and a good squeeze of lemon juice in a bowl. Season and whisk until combined, then slowly drizzle in the olive a little at a time, whisking constantly, until it has all been incorporated. Taste and add a little more lemon juice or smoked paprika according to what you like. Also, if the aïoli becomes too thick, whisk in a little warm water to loosen it slightly.

Heat the vegetable oil until it measures 180°C (350°F) on an oil thermometer. (If you don't have one of those, a cube of bread thrown in should turn golden brown in 20 seconds.)

Whisk the egg whites to stiff peaks and fold gently through the batter. Dip handfuls of courgette into the batter and fry in batches in the hot oil until golden and crispy. Drain on paper towels and keep warm while you cook the rest. Serve hot, poked upright into 12 little pots, sprinkled with sea salt, with the aïoli alongside.

GRILLED BABY LAMB CUTLETS WITH CAPONATA

Caponata is a delicious Sicilian sweet-yet-tangy vegetable dish that goes with almost anything. Enjoy hot or cold with meat, chicken or toasted ciabatta. This version is cooked so quickly that it still retains a lovely texture from the celery.

› 16 baby lamb cutlets

› 2 sprigs of rosemary, leaves picked

› extra-virgin olive oil, to marinade

› sea salt and freshly ground black pepper

› 3 tablespoons olive oil, to fry

› 1 large aubergine (eggplant), cut into 1 cm (½ in) cubes

› 1 red onion, diced

› 2 celery stalks, cut into 1 cm (½ in) cubes

› 2 garlic cloves, finely chopped

› 300 g (10½ oz/1½ cups) baby plum tomatoes, chopped

› 1 tablespoon tomato purée (paste)

› 1 tablespoon caster (superfine) sugar

› 2 tablespoons red wine vinegar

› 4 tablespoons baby capers

› 3 tablespoons toasted pine nuts

› handful of basil leaves, torn

Put the lamb cutlets in a shallow dish, sprinkle over the rosemary, a little extra-virgin olive oil and season. Cover and leave to marinate for a minimum of 25 minutes.

Add 1 tablespoon of olive oil to a large sauté pan over a medium heat and cook the aubergine until golden brown on all sides. Remove with a slotted spoon and drain on paper towels.

Add another tablespoon of olive oil to the pan over a low-medium heat. Sauté the onion until soft and translucent, add the celery and garlic and cook for a further 5 minutes. Add the tomatoes, purée, sugar and vinegar and cook for 10 minutes or until the tomatoes have broken down to create a thick sauce.

Return the aubergine to the pan along with the capers, pine nuts and basil. Remove from the heat.

Heat a large frying pan over a medium-high heat with the remaining oil. Remove the lamb from the marinade and cook in batches for 2–3 minutes on each side, depending on size. Allow each batch to rest for 5 minutes and keep warm until all the lamb has been cooked. Place a heaped tablespoon of caponata on 16 small dishes and lay a lamb cutlet on top to serve.

CHICKEN POLPETTE WITH SAFFRON ORZO

This lighter version of polpette made with chicken works really well with the saffron orzo (risoni). Kids absolutely love this, because the flavours are mellow; get them involved with the rolling of the polpette.

› 400 g (14 oz/1¾ cups) minced (ground) chicken
› 3 tablespoons flat-leaf parsley leaves, finely chopped
› 40 g (1½ oz/½ cup) grated Parmesan, plus more to serve
› finely grated zest of 1 lemon
› 1 egg, lightly beaten
› 60 g (2 oz/¾ cup) fresh breadcrumbs
› sea salt and freshly ground black pepper
› 1 tablespoon olive oil
› 100 ml (3½ fl oz) fresh chicken stock

SAFFRON ORZO
› 80 g (3 oz/6 tablespoons) unsalted butter
› 2 banana shallots, finely chopped
› 2 garlic cloves, finely chopped
› 300 g (10½ oz/1½ cups) orzo
› pinch of saffron
› 1 litre (34 fl oz) hot chicken stock
› 2 tablespoons oregano leaves, chopped, plus sprigs to garnish

Place the chicken, parsley, Parmesan, lemon zest, egg, breadcrumbs and seasoning into a large bowl and massage the meat with your hands until well combined.

Take small amounts of the mixture and roll into 24 small walnut-sized balls. Cover and refrigerate for 1 hour to firm up.

Meanwhile, for the orzo, melt half the butter in a saucepan, add the shallots and cook over a medium heat until softened. Add the garlic, cook for a further minute, then tip in the orzo and stir well to coat each grain. Add the saffron, then a ladle of stock, stirring well until all the liquid has been absorbed. Repeat until all the stock has been used and the pasta is creamy and cooked al dente. Remove from the heat and stir in the oregano and remaining butter.

Place a large sauté pan over a medium-high heat, add the olive oil and the polpette and cook until golden brown all over. Add the chicken stock and bring up to a simmer, then reduce the heat and cook for 6–7 minutes or until the polpette are cooked through.

Serve a spoonful of orzo in individual dishes or on spoons, top with a polpette and garnish with a little Parmesan and a sprig of oregano.

CHOPPED CHICKEN LIVER CROSTINI
WITH BALSAMIC SHALLOTS

If you love chicken liver pâté, you are going to adore this recipe. The Italian version is a little more rustic but it's packed full of flavour.

› a knob of butter
› 2 tablespoons olive oil
› 2 shallots, finely sliced
› 80 g (2½ oz/ ½ cup) pancetta, finely chopped
› 2 garlic cloves, chopped
› 500 g (1 lb 2 oz/2 cups) chicken livers
› 2 tablespoons brandy
› 2 tablespoons dry marsala
› 2 tablespoons baby capers
› 4 tablespoons double (heavy) cream
› 2 tablespoons flat-leaf parsley, chopped, plus more to garnish
› 2 tablespoons oregano leaves, chopped
› sea salt and freshly ground black pepper
› 1 baguette, sliced and lightly toasted

BALSAMIC SHALLOTS

› 1 tablespoon olive oil
› 4 banana shallots, sliced
› 2 tablespoons caster (superfine) sugar
› 3 tablespoons red wine vinegar
› 1 tablespoon balsamic vinegar

Melt the butter with the oil in a large frying pan, add the shallots and pancetta and cook over a medium-high heat until the pancetta is crisp. Add the garlic and chicken livers and cook for 2–3 minutes or until the chicken livers have browned on each side, seasoning well. Deglaze the pan with the brandy and marsala. Allow the alcohol to reduce completely before stirring though the capers, cream and herbs. Remove from the heat, mix well and allow to cool.

For the balsamic shallots, pour the oil into a medium frying pan, add the shallots and cook over a low heat until softened. Increase the heat to medium and add the sugar and vinegars, and mix until the sugar has dissolved and the onions are coated in a syrupy glaze.

Scoop out the livers from the cooled mix. If you want the mixture coarse, roughly chop them, keeping it chunky. For a smoother consistency, pulse-blend the mixture in a food processor. Pile the chopped chicken livers on to the toasted baguette slices and add a few balsamic onions to each. Sprinkle with flat-leaf parsley and a little extra black pepper and serve with a glass of Chianti.

SWISS CHARD GNUDI

Gnudi is a soft dumpling sometimes described as 'nude' ravioli as it isn't contained in a pillow of pasta. It's just the filling, rolled and poached. This version is served with a nutty sage-infused butter.

› sea salt
› **500 g (1 lb 2 oz/3 cups) Swiss chard (silverbeet), leaves only**
› **250 g (9 oz/1 cup) ricotta**
› **1 whole egg and 1 egg yolk, lightly beaten**
› **grating of nutmeg**
› **50 g (2 oz/⅔ cup) grated Parmesan, plus extra shavings to serve**
› **freshly ground black pepper**
› **3 tablespoons '00' flour**
› **50 g (2 oz/⅓ cup) fine semolina**
› **200 g (7 oz/¾ cup) unsalted butter**
› **leaves from 1 bunch of sage**
› **50 g (2 oz/⅓ cup) toasted pine nuts**

Bring a large pan of salted water to the boil and cook the chard leaves for 4–5 minutes. Drain well and refresh in ice-cold water. When cool, drain again and squeeze out all excess moisture. Place into a food processor and finely chop the leaves, then transfer to a large bowl. Add the ricotta, eggs, nutmeg, Parmesan and seasoning, mix well and taste. Sprinkle over the '00' flour and mix again.

Divide the mixture into small walnut-sized balls. Sprinkle with the semolina and place into the fridge to firm up for 2 hours.

Bring a large pan of salted water to the boil, reduce to a simmer and then – working quickly – shake off any excess flour from the gnudi and cook in batches for 2–3 minutes, or until they float to the surface.

Meanwhile, melt the butter in a frying pan until foaming and beginning to brown. Add the sage and pine nuts, stir well and remove from the heat.

Place the gnudi on serving plates or flat spoons. Spoon over the nutty herb-infused butter and garnish each with a sage leaf. Sprinkle with Parmesan shavings and serve.

CAREY'S BABY OCTOPUS SALAD

I learnt the recipe for this tangy, crunchy salad from my beloved mentor Carey Terranova. Be sure not to overcook the octopus — you want a lovely soft texture. This will keep in the fridge for up to a week as long as it's submerged in the marinade.

› 1 litre (34 fl oz) vegetable stock
› 1¼ kg (2 lb 10 oz) baby octopus, cleaned and beaks removed
› 350 ml (11½ fl oz) extra-virgin olive oil, plus more if needed
› 75 ml (2½ fl oz) red wine vinegar
› 75 ml (2½ fl oz) white wine vinegar
› 2 garlic cloves, finely sliced
› 1 long red chilli, deseeded and finely sliced
› ½ red onion, finely sliced
› 1 carrot, finely chopped
› 2 celery stalks, finely sliced
› ½ teaspoon dried oregano
› leaves from 2 sprigs of oregano
› 1 teaspoon fennel seeds
› 1 bay leaf
› finely grated zest of 1 lemon
› sea salt and freshly ground black pepper
› flat-leaf parsley, finely chopped, to serve
› lemon wedges, to serve (optional)

Bring the vegetable stock to the boil in a saucepan. Add the octopus, return to the boil and cook for 10–12 minutes or until tender.

Drain and transfer the warm octopus to a large glass or ceramic bowl. Add the oil, vinegars, garlic, chilli, red onion, carrot, celery, both types of oregano, fennel seeds, bay leaf, lemon zest and seasoning. Stir well to combine, making sure the octopus is completely submerged in the pickling liquid. Add more olive oil if you need to. Cover and refrigerate for a minimum of 24 hours. When you are ready to serve, stir through the parsley.

Serve spoonfuls of the salad on 8 dishes, with a few toothpicks alongside and lemon wedges, if you want.

MINI VEAL MILANESE <u>WITH</u> GIARDINIERA TARTARE

Giardiniera is a delicious blend of Italian pickled vegetables and I first learned how to make into this delicious tartare sauce when I was an apprentice chef. It's my favourite tartare to this day.

› 1 x 500 g (1 lb 2 oz) piece of veal, topside
› sea salt and freshly ground black pepper
› 200 g (7 oz/1½ cups) plain (all-purpose) flour
› 2 eggs, lightly beaten
› 250 g (9 oz/2½ cups) panko (Japanese style) breadcrumbs
› 2 tablespoons flat-leaf parsley leaves, finely chopped
  2 tablespoons vegetable oil, to shallow-fry
› tiny lemon wedges, to serve

GIARDINIERA TARTARE

› 100 g (3½ oz/⅓ cup) giardiniera vegetables, finely chopped
› 75 g (2½ oz/⅓ cup) mayonnaise
› 2 tablespoons flat-leaf parsley leaves, finely chopped
› juice of 1 lemon
› ½ small red onion, finely sliced
› 2 baby fennel bulbs, finely sliced
› leaves from 2 sprigs of dill, to serve

Season the veal with salt and pepper and cut into 24 even-sized chunks. Pound each chunk with a rolling pin or meat mallet until thin. Don't worry if they are all slightly different shapes, it will add to their charm! Season the flour well and then put the flour, eggs and breadcrumbs in three separate bowls. Roll each piece of veal in flour, dip in egg and then coat in panko crumbs.

Make the tartare by mixing together the giardiniera, mayonnaise, parsley and half the lemon juice together. Pour the remaining lemon juice into a separate bowl and add the red onion, fennel and dill. Season lightly and stir together.

Heat the vegetable oil in a large frying pan and cook the mini veal Milanese in batches, making sure you don't crowd the pan. Drain on paper towels and keep warm until all the veal has been cooked. Lay on a platter and top with a small dollop of tartare and a little of the fennel mixture. Serve topped with tiny lemon wedges and the extra tartare sauce on the side.

SPRITZ ME UP BABY

The humble Aperol spritz is my all-time favourite drink. But I think it's time to add another level to it. Aperol is made from bitter oranges and rhubarb, so how better to serve it than with a refreshing rhubarb sorbet.

RHUBARB SORBET

› **500 g (1 lb 2 oz/4 cups) rhubarb, chopped into 2½ cm (1 in) lengths**
› **250 g (9 oz/1¼ cup) caster (superfine) sugar**
› **100 ml (3½ fl oz) grenadine**
› **finely grated zest and juice of 1 orange**
› **finely grated zest and juice of 1 lemon**
› **juice of 1 pink grapefruit**
› **1 tablespoon finely grated fresh ginger**

APEROL SPRITZ

› **300 ml (½ pint) Aperol**
› **100 ml (3½ fl oz) gin (for an extra kick)**
› **600 ml (1 pint) Prosecco**
› **orange slices and orange zest curls, to garnish (optional)**

Begin by making the sorbet. Put all the ingredients into a medium saucepan with 400 ml (13 fl oz) of water. Set over a medium heat and stir until the sugar has dissolved. Simmer for 10 minutes, or until the rhubarb is very soft. Carefully transfer the mixture to a food processor and blend until smooth. Pass the purée through a fine sieve, making sure to push down on the pulp to extract as much liquid as possible. Leave to cool completely before pouring it into an ice-cream maker to churn. When it's nearly set, transfer to freezerproof containers and place in the freezer for 2–3 hours to set completely. Place 6 serving glasses into the freezer, too.

Take a cocktail shaker or jug and fill halfway with ice. Pour in the Aperol, gin and Prosecco and stir well. Remove the glasses from the freezer and fill each three-quarters full with the spritz. Working quickly, put a scoop of sorbet in each glass, add an orange slice and an orange zest curl, if you like, and serve immediately with a small spoon.

BOOZY TIRAMISU POTS

These are gorgeous: both light and indulgent. The word 'tiramisu' actually means 'pick me up' and these boozy versions will be sure to do just that.

› **350 ml (11½ fl oz) very strong espresso**
› **2 tablespoons agave syrup or demerara (turbinado) sugar**
› **3 tablespoons Disaronno (almond liqueur)**
› **3 tablespoons coffee liqueur**
› **6 free-range eggs, separated**
› **200 g (7 oz/1 cup) golden caster (unrefined superfine) sugar**
› **120 ml (4 fl oz) marsala**
› **500 g (1 lb 2 oz/2¼ cups) mascarpone, lightly whipped**
› **40 savoiardi (ladyfingers) biscuits**
› **cocoa powder, to serve**

First sweeten the coffee by stirring through the agave syrup (the caramel tones work beautifully with coffee), or heat the coffee and dissolve the demerara in it. Add both liqueurs, stir well and allow to cool.

Whisk the eggs whites to stiff peaks. Put the egg yolks and sugar in a bowl and whisk with electric beaters for 5 minutes, or until pale and thick. Continue whisking and gradually add the marsala a little at a time until it has been incorporated. Fold in the mascarpone, then fold in the egg whites as gently as possible, to keep the mixture light.

Lay 20 glasses out ready. Dunk one biscuit into the coffee mixture until it's completely soaked without it being so soft that it falls apart in your hands. Break in half and lay one half in a glass. Add a heaped tablespoon of the mascarpone mixture, then the other half of the biscuit and another tablespoon of mascarpone. Sift over a little cocoa and repeat the layers until all the glasses are full. Cover each pot with plastic wrap and refrigerate for a few hours, or overnight, to set.

When you are ready to serve, sprinkle lots of cocoa over each tiramisu.

CHOCOLATE 'SALAMI'

I just love the way you can have fun with the presentation of this. (I always add a little name tag, just so people know what it is!) So simple to make, but be sure to give it the full three hours to firm up to avoid it being too crumbly.

- › 200 g (7 oz/1¼ cups) dark (bittersweet) chocolate, broken up
- › 100 g (3½ oz/1 stick) butter, softened
- › 120 g (4 oz/½ cup) caster (superfine) sugar
- › 2 medium eggs
- › 2 tablespoons Disaronno (almond liqueur), or hazelnut liqueur, or brandy
- › 200 g (7 oz/3 cups) crunchy amaretti biscuits (or your favourite type), slightly crushed
- › 50 g (2 oz/⅓ cup) pistachios
- › 50 g (2 oz/⅓ cup) almonds
- › 50 g (2 oz/⅓ cup) hazelnuts
- › 50 g (2 oz/⅓ cup) dried sour cherries
- › cocoa powder, to dust
- › icing (confectioners') sugar, to dust
- › butcher's string, for presentation

Melt the chocolate in a heatproof bowl over a pan of gently simmering water, making sure the bowl does not touch the water. Set aside to cool slightly. Meanwhile cream the butter and sugar together using an electric whisk until the mixture is pale and fluffy. Beat in the eggs one at a time and then add the liqueur. Stir in the cooled chocolate and add the biscuits, nuts and sour cherries. Fold the chocolate mixture gently over the dry ingredients, making sure to coat them well.

Now take 2 large pieces of plastic wrap and lay another layer of plastic wrap over each one so you have 2 doubled layers. If the chocolate mixture is too soft, place it in the fridge for 10 minutes to help it firm up a little. Divide the mixture into 2 and place one on each of the layers of plastic wrap. Wet your hands a little and mould each piece of mixture into a log around 20 cm (8 in) long and 2½ cm (1 in) wide, tapering at each end (this is where you will tie the string around it later). Wrap with the plastic wrap, twisting each end like a Christmas cracker. Refrigerate for 3 hours to firm up.

When you are ready to serve, remove the plastic wrap and lay the 'salamis' on some baking paper. Dust with cocoa and icing sugar and wrap some string around each log at 2½ cm (1 in) intervals, to make it look like a real salami. Slice and serve on a board, leaving the knife there for people to cut more slices as they wish.

MINI FIG, ALMOND <u>AND</u> HONEY CAKES

Wait for it... Yes, these little cakes are wheat free. And they are a perfect sweet finish with a hint of orange.

CAKES

› **150 g (5 oz/½ cup) butter, softened, plus extra for the cake moulds**
› **150 g (5 oz/¾ cup) golden caster (unrefined superfine) sugar**
› **3 eggs, lightly beaten**
› **finely grated zest of 1 orange**
› **3 tablespoons honey**
› **200 g (7 oz/2 cups) ground almonds (almond meal)**
› **3 figs, quartered**

CARAMEL FIGS

› **2 tablespoons butter**
› **juice of 1 orange**
› **4 tablespoons honey**
› **6 figs, quartered**

Preheat the oven to 180°C (350°F/Gas 4). Butter each of 12 fairy cake or mini muffin moulds with a pastry brush and line the bases with a small round of baking paper.

Cream together the butter and sugar with electric beaters until pale and fluffy, then add the eggs gradually until incorporated. Now fold in the orange zest, honey and ground almonds.

Divide the mixture between the moulds and place in the oven for 8–10 minutes or until the cake begins to set around the edges.

Remove from the oven and poke a fig quarter into the middle of each cake. Return to the oven for a further 10–12 minutes or until risen and golden. Leave to cool for 5 minutes before turning them out on to a wire rack.

For the caramel figs, heat the butter in a frying pan over a medium heat, add the orange juice and honey, and allow to bubble and thicken. Add the figs and toss in the honey syrup for 2 minutes. Remove from heat and top each cake with figs and some syrup while they are still warm. Serve immediately.

LIMONE <u>AND</u> MINT SORBET

A great dairy-free alternative to gelato. This is so refreshing and can also be mixed with Prosecco and a dash of elderflower syrup to be turned into yet another great cocktail...

› **300 g (10½ oz/1⅓ cups) caster (superfine) sugar**
› **finely grated zest of 2 lemons, plus lemon zest curls to serve**
› **leaves from 4 sprigs of mint, chopped, plus more to serve**
› **140 ml (4½ fl oz) lemon juice**
› **lemon shells to serve**

Combine the sugar, lemon zest, mint leaves and 500 ml (17 fl oz) of water in a saucepan and set over a low heat, stirring occasionally until the sugar dissolves. Allow the mixture to simmer for 5 minutes. Remove from the heat and stir in the lemon juice. Strain the syrup through a sieve then leave to cool completely. Pour it into an ice cream maker to churn. When it's nearly set, transfer to freezerproof containers and freeze for 2–3 hours to set completely.

If you haven't cracked the skins of the lemons too much when squeezing them for the juice, you can use the shells to serve. Simply scrape out any remaining flesh with a teaspoon and trim off the end to make a flat surface. Scoop out large balls of sorbet and place inside of each hollowed-out lemon half.

Keep in the freezer until ready to serve. Garnish with a tiny mint sprig and lemon zest curls.

BOMBOLONI

These are the softest, cloud-like mini Italian doughnuts. I dare you to try to stop at just one. Don't worry though, this recipe makes so many, you won't have to.

DOUGHNUTS

› **2 sachets (14 g/½ oz) of dried yeast**
› **280 ml (9 fl oz) warm milk**
› **70 g (2¼ oz/⅓ cup) caster (superfine) sugar**
› **560 g (1 lb 4 oz/4½ cups) plain (all-purpose) flour, plus more to dust**
› **pinch of sea salt**
› **8 large egg yolks**
› **1 teaspoon finely grated lemon zest**
› **1 teaspoon finely grated orange zest**
› **100 g (3½ oz/⅓ cup) butter, melted**
› **vegetable oil, to deep-fry**

COATING AND FILLING

› **200 g (7 oz/1 cup) caster (superfine) sugar**
› **2 teaspoons ground cinnamon**
› **Nutella, to fill**
› **raspberry jam, to fill**

Mix the yeast with half the milk and 1 tablespoon of both the sugar and the flour. Leave for 10 minutes to allow the yeast to activate. Mix the remaining flour and sugar in a large bowl and make a well in the centre. Pour in the yeast mixture and add the salt, egg yolks and zests. Gradually mix the flour from the outside into the wet mix until combined to form a dough. Place the dough on a lightly floured surface, knead well for a few minutes, then flatten and make a well in the centre. Pour the melted butter in the well and fold the dough towards the centre to incorporate all the butter. Place in a floured bowl and leave in a warm place to rise for 1 hour. Line a baking tray with baking paper and sprinkle it with flour.

Remove the risen dough from the bowl and place on a lightly floured surface. Roll out to ½ cm (¼ in) thick and, using a 2½ cm (1 in) round cookie cutter, cut out rounds and place them on the prepared tray. Heat the oil one-third up the sides, in a deep pan to 170°C (340°F). Carefully drop in a few of the bomboloni. Cook for 2–3 minutes on each side, making sure to turn them once. Drain them on paper towels and cook the rest.

For the coating, mix together the sugar and cinnamon in a bowl. While the bomboloni are still warm, toss them in the bowl. Fill a squeezy bottle or a piping bag with Nutella or raspberry jam. Poke a hole through each bomboloni and squeeze the filling into each one. Serve warm.

BELLINI SLUSH

Peaches and Prosecco are a marriage made in heaven. Here is a simple way to join them together for a refreshing, elegant dessert.

› **200 g (7 oz/1 cup) caster (superfine) sugar**
› **juice of 1 lemon**
› **750 g (1 lb 10 oz) ripe peaches (white are best here, if in season), plus 3 peaches, sliced, to serve**
› **750 ml (25 fl oz) Prosecco**
› **pink rose petals or mint leaves, to garnish (optional)**

Put the sugar and lemon juice in a saucepan with 300 ml (half a pint) of water. Stir over a low heat until the sugar dissolves, then allow to cool.

Next prepare the 750 g (1 lb 10 oz) of peaches by removing the skins and stones. Put the flesh in a food processor and blend until smooth. Mix the peach purée with the sugar syrup and half the Prosecco, pour into a shallow freezerproof container, cover and freeze for 2 hours. Now gently scrape the frozen edges, using a fork, every 30 minutes or so until the whole mixture turns to frozen crystals.

Place a couple of slices of peach in the base of 8 glasses. Spoon the slush over and garnish with a couple more slices of peach and a few rose petals or mint leaves, if you like. Pour a little of the remaining Prosecco over the frozen mixture and serve immediately.

CINNAMON AND MASCARPONE GELATO WITH SALTED CARAMEL

This is simply the richest, creamiest, most voluptuous ice cream I have ever made. The salted caramel swirl makes it truly sublime.

GELATO

› **250 g (9 oz/1 cup) mascarpone**
› **250 ml (8½ fl oz) double (heavy) cream**
› **250 ml (8½ fl oz) whole milk**
› **1 cinnamon stick, plus more to garnish (optional)**
› **5 egg yolks**
› **100 g (3½ oz/½ cup) golden caster (unrefined superfine) sugar**
› **½ teaspoon ground cinnamon**

SALTED CARAMEL

› **125 g (4 oz/⅔ cup) caster (superfine) sugar**
› **200 ml (7 fl oz) double (heavy) cream**
› **½ teaspoon sea salt flakes**
› **1 teaspoon vanilla extract**

Put the mascarpone, cream, milk and cinnamon stick into a saucepan and gently heat to a simmer. Remove from the heat and leave to infuse for 15 minutes.

Whisk the egg yolks, sugar and cinnamon in a large bowl until pale and fluffy. Remove the cinnamon stick from the mascarpone mixture and pour it gradually into the egg mixture, until incorporated. Return to the pan and stir gently over a low-medium heat until it thickens enough to coat the back of a spoon. Remove from the heat and allow to cool completely. When cool, pour it into an ice-cream maker to churn.

To make the salted caramel, place the sugar and 4 tablespoons of water into a saucepan. Set over a high heat (without stirring) until it reaches a deep caramel colour. Remove from the heat and carefully add the cream as it will splatter. Now stir over a medium heat until all the caramel has dissolved once more. Stir in the salt and vanilla and leave to cool completely.

When the ice cream has nearly set, transfer to a freezerproof container, drizzling the cooled salted caramel over after every 2 spoonfuls or so. Run a blunt knife through the ice cream to create more of a swirl. Freeze for 2–3 hours to set completely. Scoop small balls of ice cream and serve in mini ice cream cones or small bowls. Garnish with cinnamon sticks.

ESPRESSO MARTINI GRANITA CUPS

A refreshing change to the usual espresso martini, but with all the delicious flavour. It might seem like a lot of booze ... but once you taste it, I'm sure you'll agree it's just right.

› **600 ml (1 pint) hot espresso**
› **150 g (5 oz/¾ cup) demerara (turbinado) sugar**
› **150 ml (5 fl oz) vodka**
› **3½ tablespoons Disaronno (almond liqueur)**
› **3½ tablespoons coffee liqueur**
› **1½ tablespoons orange liqueur**
› **300 ml (½ pint) double (heavy) cream**
› **1 vanilla pod, seeds scraped out**
› **3½ tablespoons caster (superfine) sugar**
› **coffee beans to decorate**

While the espresso is hot, mix in the sugar until it has completely dissolved. Add the vodka and liqueurs and allow the mixture to cool down completely. Pour into a deep freezerproof tray that will fit into and freeze. After 30 minutes, fork through the outside frozen layers, moving them to the centre, and return to the freezer. Repeat this process every 30 minutes or so until you are left with a tray of slushy crystals.

Meanwhile, whip the cream with the vanilla seeds and caster sugar.

When the granita is ready, spoon it into 10 small decorative glasses. Top with a dollop of the sweetened vanilla cream and decorate with a few crushed espresso beans.

BACI DI DAMA (LADIES' KISSES)

There's a lovely chocolate-filled biscuit in Australia called Kingston (a big childhood favourite of mine), and these little beauties are the Italian equivalent. Nutty, crunchy, chocolatey goodness.

› **120 g (4 oz/1 cup) blanched hazelnuts, toasted**
› **160 g (5½ oz/1¼ cups) icing (confectioners') sugar**
› **125 g (4½ oz/½ cup) butter, softened**
› **finely grated zest of 1 small orange**
› **160 g (5½ oz/1¼ cups) plain (all-purpose) flour**
› **150 g (5 oz/½ cup) Nutella**

Preheat the oven to 180°C (350°F/Gas 4). Line a baking tray with baking paper.

Place the hazelnuts and sugar into a food processor and blend until the nuts are finely ground.

Place this mixture into a large bowl with the butter and orange zest. Using electric beaters, whisk well. Gently fold in the flour until it's just combined.

Roll half teaspoons of the mixture into balls and place on the baking tray, spaced about 5 cm (2 in) apart. Bake for 12–15 minutes or until golden and crispy. When cooled slightly, gently transfer them to a wire rack to cool down completely.

Add a little dollop of Nutella over the flat side of each biscuit and press another biscuit on top, flat sides together.

Serve with coffee.

MINI CROSTATE DI FRUTTA

Tiny versions of a classic Italian dessert spiked with a little limoncello and a selection of delicious fruit. Get involved!

› **250 ml (8½ fl oz) whole milk**
› **pared zest of 1 lemon**
› **1 vanilla pod, seeds scraped out**
› **5 egg yolks**
› **5 tablespoons caster (superfine) sugar**
› **3½ tablespoons cornflour (cornstarch)**
› **3½ tablespoons limoncello (lemon liqueur)**
› **100 ml (3½ fl oz) double (heavy) cream, softly whipped**
› **24 mini sweet shortcrust tartlet cases**
› **600 g (1 lb 5 oz/5 cups) assorted mixed fruit, such as strawberries, peaches, raspberries, blueberries, apricots, kiwi fruit, blackberries or grapes**
› **3 tablespoons apricot or apple jam**

Heat up the milk, lemon zest and vanilla seeds until the mixture just begins to boil, then remove from the heat. Separately beat the egg yolks and sugar until pale and fluffy. Stir in the cornflour and one-third of the hot milk, whisking constantly. Whisk in the remaining milk, then return to the pan. Cook over a low heat, stirring constantly with the whisk, for 8–10 minutes. Once the mixture begins to thicken, remove from the heat. Add the limoncello, cover with plastic wrap and leave to cool completely.

Once cooled, fold in the whipped cream and spoon the mixture into a piping bag. Snip the end off and pipe a small amount into each tartlet case.

Slice all the fruits so the pieces are small enough to fit into the tartlet cases. Top each tart with the assorted fruit.

Heat up the jam with 3 tablespoons of water until the jam dissolves. Strain the mixture into a separate small bowl and brush a little of this glaze over the fruit on each tartlet, for a beautiful shine.

MINI RICOTTA-FILLED CANNOLI

You can purchase mini cannoli shells online or from great Italian delis. Then all you need to do is make the filling and jazz them up with melted chocolate and nuts.

FILLING

› **350 g (12 oz/1⅓ cups) ricotta**
› **80 g (3 oz/⅓ cup) caster (superfine) sugar**
› **40 g (1½ oz/¼ cup) dark chocolate, finely chopped**
› **50 g (2 oz/⅓ cup) candied orange peel, finely chopped**
› **finely grated zest of 1 orange**

TO ASSEMBLE

› **100 g (3 ½ oz/⅔ cup) dark chocolate, broken**
› **20 mini cannoli shells**
› **50 g (2 oz/⅓ cup) hazelnuts, finely chopped**
› **50 g (2 oz/⅓ cup) pistachios, finely chopped**

Make the filling by whipping the ricotta in a bowl with electric beaters until smooth. Then mix with the sugar, chocolate, candied peel and zest. Fill the mixture into a piping bag fitted with a small star nozzle and refrigerate until needed.

To assemble, melt the chocolate in a heatproof bowl over a pan of gently simmering water, making sure the bowl does not touch the water. Take each cannoli shell and dip the ends in the melted chocolate. Then dip into either the hazelnuts or the pistachios. Allow them to dry and set. Pipe the ricotta filling into each shell and serve on a platter.

PISTACHIO <u>AND</u> ALMOND CANTUCCINI

These crunchy little treats are perfect enjoyed with a glass of Vin Santo, or a hot sweet tea or coffee. Keep them in an airtight container to enjoy at your leisure.

› **350 g (12 oz/2⅔ cups) plain (all-purpose) flour**
› **200 g (7 oz/1 cup) golden caster (unrefined superfine) sugar**
› **1 teaspoon baking powder**
› **70 g (2¼ oz/½ cup) blanched almonds, toasted**
› **70 g (2¼ oz/½ cup) pistachios**
› **70 g (2¼ oz/½ cup) dark chocolate, finely chopped**
› **1 teaspoon vanilla extract**
› **4 tablespoons butter, softened**
› **3 eggs, lightly beaten**
› **icing (confectioners') sugar, to dust**
› **melted milk and white chocolate, to dip**

Preheat the oven to 180°C (350°F/Gas 4). Line a baking tray with baking paper.

Put all the dry ingredients into a large bowl with the vanilla extract and butter. Gradually add the beaten eggs and mix with a wooden spoon until it begins to come together to form a dough. You may not need to use all the eggs.

Dust a work surface with icing sugar and divide the dough into 2 pieces. Form each piece into a log about 15 cm (6 in) long and 3½ cm (1½ in) wide. Gently flatten each log a little and place on the baking tray.

Bake for 25–30 minutes, then remove from the oven. Reduce the oven temperature to 150°C (300°F/Gas 2). Using a sharp knife, cut the log into 1 cm (½ in) slices and place back on the tray. Return to the oven for another 10–15 minutes or until lightly golden and dried out.

Dip the cantuccini in melted milk or white chocolate and allow to set before serving.

CHOCOLATE <u>AND</u> HAZELNUT GELATO

A rich indulgent adult gelato that also contains one of my favourite childhood flavours: Nutella. I could eat almost a whole jar by myself when I was younger. This recipe will be one you make again and again...

› **250 ml (8½ fl oz) whole milk**
› **125 ml (4 fl oz) double (heavy) cream**
› **100 g (3½ oz/⅓ cup) Nutella**
› **150 ml (5 fl oz) Frangelico (hazelnut liqueur)**
› **4 egg yolks**
› **5 tablespoons caster (superfine) sugar**
› **100 g (3½ oz/⅔ cup) toasted hazelnuts, finely chopped**
› **mini waffle cones or chocolate wafers, to serve**

Pour the milk and cream into a saucepan, add the Nutella and heat gently until the Nutella melts.

Meanwhile pour the Frangelico into a small saucepan, place over a high heat and reduce by half, to intensify the flavour. Remove and set aside to cool.

Whisk the egg yolks with the sugar until pale and creamy. Slowly add the milk mixture, whisking constantly. Return the mixture to the pan and stir gently over a low–medium heat until the mixture thickens enough to coat the back of a spoon.

Remove from the heat and stir in the Frangelico and half the hazelnuts, then allow to cool down completely. Pour it into an ice-cream maker to churn. When it's nearly set, transfer to freezerproof containers and freeze for 2–3 hours to set completely.

When set, using a melon baller or mini ice-cream scoop, scoop out balls and serve them in mini ice-cream cones or small bowls. You can store them in the freezer already scooped and ready to go, standing up in egg cartons as they are here. When your guests arrive and it's gelato time, grab them out of the freezer so they don't melt before you're ready.

MINI LIMONCELLO <u>AND</u> BLUEBERRY TRIFLES

If you've ever visited the Amalfi coast you have no doubt returned with a love of limoncello. This lovely light, layered dessert with blueberries showcases the drink in the most delightful way.

FRUIT AND SYRUP

› **5 tablespoons caster (superfine) sugar**
› **120 ml (4 fl oz) limoncello**
› **1 teaspoon arrowroot**
› **450 g (1 lb/2¾ cups) blueberries**

MASCARPONE MIXTURE

› **5 medium eggs, separated**
› **120 g (4 oz/⅔ cup) golden caster (unrefined superfine) sugar**
› **250 g (9 oz/1 cup) mascarpone**
› **6 tablespoons lemon curd**
› **¼ pandoro (golden cake), cut into 1 cm (½ in) slices**

TOPPING

› **400 ml (13 fl oz) double (heavy) cream, whipped**
› **finely grated zest of 1 lemon, to garnish**

For the fruit and syrup dissolve the sugar into a small pan with 300 ml (half a pint) of cold water over a medium heat and simmer gently for 5 minutes. Remove 3 tablespoons of the syrup and set aside. Stir the remainder with the limoncello and leave to cool. Mix the arrowroot with 2 tablespoons of cold water.

Pour most of the blueberries into a saucepan. (Keep a handful for the topping.) Add the reserved syrup and cook the blueberries over a medium heat for 2–3 minutes or until the blueberry colour begins to release. This mixture should be jam-like, so mash down some of the blueberries with a back of a fork to help break them down a little. Add the arrowroot mixture, stir well, remove from the heat and allow to cool.

For the mascarpone mixture, whisk the egg whites into a large clean bowl until soft peaks form. Put the egg yolks and sugar into a separate bowl and beat until pale and thick. Add the mascarpone and lemon curd and and gently fold the mixture.

Cut the pandoro into pieces that will fit into 12 mini pots or glasses and dip briefly into the limoncello syrup and place in the glasses. Top each with a spoon of mascarpone mixture and then 1 teaspoon of blueberries. Repeat with one more layer of all 3 components. Refrigerate for 2 hours to set. When you are ready to serve, top each glass with a dollop of whipped cream, a few of the reserved blueberries and some lemon zest.

STRAWBERRY SORBET-FILLED PISTACHIO KISSES

Strawberries and meringue made into the perfect little mouthful. These are a bit fiddly to assemble but well worth the time. The pistachios add a lovely crunch.

STRAWBERRY SORBET

› **500 g (1 lb 2 oz/3 ⅓ cups) strawberries, hulled**
› **70 ml (3 fl oz) liquid glucose**
› **2 tablespoons icing (confectioners') sugar**
› **1 vanilla pod, seeds scraped out**
› **juice of ½ lemon**

PISTACHIO KISSES

› **3 egg whites**
› **100 g (3½ oz/½ cup) caster (superfine) sugar**
› **5 tablespoons icing (confectioners') sugar**
› **70 g (2¼ oz/¾ cup) ground pistachios**

Tip the strawberries into a food processor and blend until smooth. Pass the purée through a fine sieve, pushing down on the pulp to extract as much juice as possible. Pour the strawberry juice into a small saucepan with the glucose, sugar and vanilla seeds. Stir over a gentle heat until the sugar has dissolved. Remove from the heat and stir in the lemon juice. Leave to cool completely before pouring into an ice-cream maker to churn. When it's nearly set, transfer to freezerproof containers and freeze for 2–3 hours to set completely.

For the pistachio kisses, preheat the oven to 110°C (225°F/Gas ¼). Whisk the egg whites in a large bowl to form soft peaks. Gradually whisk in the sugar, then the icing sugar, whisking until the meringue is firm and glossy. Fold in half the ground pistachios.

Take a little of the meringue mixture and drop a small blob in the corners of a baking tray. Place a piece of baking paper on top and press the corners down well. Spoon the remaining mixture into a piping bag fitted with a small plain nozzle. Pipe mini swirled meringues evenly on the baking paper until all the meringue is used up. Sprinkle the remaining pistachios on top of the kisses, then bake for 40 minutes or until crisp. Remove from the oven and allow to cool completely.

Sandwich a small scoop of sorbet between 2 kisses. Place in the freezer as you make them until you are ready to serve.

PEACH ZABAGLIONE

This is a gently cooked custard that is whipped constantly to incorporate as much air as possible to give you an extremely light consistency. It's a classic and absolutely delicious.

› **10 large egg yolks**
› **250 g (9 oz/1¼ cups) caster (superfine) sugar**
› **350 ml (11 fl oz) dry marsala**
› **6 yellow-fleshed peaches**
› **6 amaretti biscuits, crushed**

Place the egg yolks, sugar and marsala into a large heatproof bowl over a pan of gentle simmering water. Whisk with electric beaters, as it will take around 15 minutes for the mixture to become, pale, thick and triple in volume.

Remove the bowl from the heat and continue whisking until the mixture cools down a little. Cut the peaches in half, remove the stones, then cut each half into thin wedges. Place a few slices in the bottom of 8 to 10 glasses. Sprinkle over some of the amaretti crumbs and top with the zabaglione mixture. Add a few more peach slices and amaretti crumbs. Serve straight away.

CARAMEL BUDINO

This is the Italian version of a crème caramel. For a special twist, top each with chocolate curls for a little extra indulgence.

BUDINO

› **500 ml (17 fl oz) whole milk**
› **1 vanilla pod, seeds scraped out**
› **3 tablespoons espresso**
› **3 large eggs, plus 1 large egg yolk**
› **100 g (3½ oz/½ cup) golden caster (unrefined superfine) sugar**

CARAMEL

› **225 g (8 oz/1¼ cups) golden caster (unrefined superfine) sugar**
› **3 tablespoons marsala**

Preheat the oven to 140°C (275°F/Gas 1).

Begin the budino by heating the milk, vanilla seeds and espresso in a pan until it nearly comes to a simmer. Place the eggs, extra yolk and sugar into a bowl and whisk until pale, then gradually whisk in the warm milk until combined.

Next make the caramel: put the sugar and 3 tablespoons of water into a deep saucepan. Allow the sugar to melt and turn a deep golden colour; do not stir. Remove from the heat and carefully add the marsala, standing back as it will splatter a little. While the caramel is still warm, divide it between 10 x 90 ml (3 fl oz) mini pudding moulds.

Place the moulds into a roasting tray. Fill the tray with hot water until the water reaches 2 cm (¾ in) up the side of each mould. Place carefully into the oven and cook for 40 minutes, or until the custard is just set.

Leave to cool, then refrigerate for 2–3 hours or overnight. The longer you leave them the more caramel will release when they are unmoulded. When you are ready to serve, unmould them by running a sharp knife around the edges of each mould, then pressing them gently with your fingers to loosen. Tip each over on to a plate and allow the caramel sauce to flow around.

MINI LEMON PANNA COTTA POTS WITH RHUBARB AND RASPBERRIES

Panna cotta simply means 'cooked cream'. These can be topped with almost anything, so experiment with different fruits. The silky, sexy dessert is sure to impress.

PANNA COTTA POTS

› **1 litre (34 fl oz) double (heavy) cream**
› **300 ml (½ pint) whole milk**
› **pared zest of 1 lemon**
› **1 vanilla pod, seeds scraped out**
› **3 gelatine leaves**
› **150 g (5 oz/1¼ cups) icing (confectioners') sugar**

RHUBARB AND RASPBERRY COMPOTE

› **6 rhubarb stalks, cut into 5 cm (2 in) lengths**
› **150 g (5 oz/¾ cup) caster (superfine) sugar**
› **4 tablespoons grenadine syrup**
› **200 ml (7 fl oz) Moscato d'Asti, or other semi-sweet sparkling white wine**
› **150 g (5 oz/1¼ cups) raspberries**

Place the cream, milk, lemon zest and vanilla seeds in a saucepan and bring to the simmer. Simmer for around 10 minutes or until the mixture has reduced by one-third.

Meanwhile place the gelatine leaves in a bowl of cold water to soften. Remove the cream mixture from the heat and whisk in the sugar until it dissolves. Leave until it is just hand-hot, then squeeze the excess water from the gelatine and whisk that in, too. Allow to cool completely.

Ladle the mixture into 12 small jars or glasses, to fill each two-thirds full. Cover with plastic wrap and place into the fridge to set.

For the compote: preheat the oven to 170°C (340°F/Gas 3½). Put the rhubarb, sugar, grenadine and wine into a shallow baking tray. Place in the oven for 15 minutes, or until the rhubarb is just cooked but still holding its shape. Keep an eye on it as you don't want it to overcook. Leave to cool. When ready to serve, gently stir through the raspberries.

Divide the rhubarb mixture between the small jars or glasses of panna cotta, making sure to pour a little of the poaching liquor over too.

AMARETTO AFFOGATO SHOTS

These can be enjoyed at any time of the day. If you fancy a lovely caffeine hit with a little extra kick, this is for you.

› **600 ml (1 pint) vanilla ice cream**
› **150 ml (5 fl oz) Disaronno (almond liqueur)**
› **350 ml (11½ fl oz) hot espresso**
› **20 amaretti biscuits, to serve (optional)**

Using a small ice-cream scoop or melon baller, scoop 20 small or 10 medium balls of ice cream and lay them on a baking tray lined with baking paper. Return to the freezer for about 1 hour. This will ensure they don't melt too quickly when the hot coffee hits them.

Mix the liqueur and coffee together and divide between 10 small glasses or espresso cups. Gently add a medium scoop or 2 small scoops of ice cream and serve immediately with the amaretti biscuits alongside.

If you wish, you can put the ice cream straight into the serving glasses, freeze, then remove them, pour the coffee over and serve. If you want to do it this way, the serving glasses will have to be thick and robust, otherwise they might crack.

INDEX

ACKNOWLEDGEMENTS

I'd like to give special thanks to my family for always supporting my passion for food and allowing me to follow my dreams.

I'd also like to thank Kate Pollard for giving me the opportunity to write this book. And to my DREAM TEAM: the lovely and talented Jacqui Melville behind the camera that has worked her magic yet again; the delightful Jessica Mills who has been my great friend and assistant for years now and to April Carter for lending a helping hand at the last minute. I couldn't have done it without you all.

And lastly to my second father Carey, thank you for everything. I wouldn't be the chef or woman that I am now if we had never met. Even though you are no longer with us, you will remain in my heart always. I dedicate this book to you.

ABOUT THE AUTHOR

Nicole Herft's passion for food began at the tender age of seven when her mother handed her her very first cookbook. Soon after she became addicted to cooking, eating, and all things food. To be honest, not much has changed since!

After finishing high school, Nicole stumbled on a part-time job at the local Italian restaurant. Here she met her beloved first mentor, Carey Terranova, and decided to take on an apprenticeship to become a chef. At 22 she moved to London tocontinue her cooking career and embark on many travel adventures.

These days, Nicole works as a food stylist for TV, magazines and cookbooks. She has worked with many of the industry greats, including Ina Garten on her Barefoot Contessa *TV show, Gordon Ramsay, Tom Kerridge, Jason Atherton and with the team on BBC One's* Saturday Kitchen. *She remains a serial entertainer who loves to serve inventive and delicious food to her guests in her flat in London.*

Follow her travel and eating adventures on twitter:
https://twitter.com/Eat_Love_Travel

Little Italy by Nicole Herft

First published in 2014 by Hardie Grant Books

Hardie Grant Books (UK)
Dudley House, North Suite
34–35 Southampton Street
London WC2E 7HF
www.hardiegrant.co.uk

Hardie Grant Books (Australia)
Ground Floor, Building 1
658 Church Street
Melbourne, VIC 3121
www.hardiegrant.com.au

British Library Cataloguing-in-Publication Data. A catalogue
record for this book is available from the British Library.

ISBN 978-174270-771-6

Publisher: Kate Pollard
Desk Editor: Kajal Mistry
Cover and Internal Design: Julia Murray
Photographer: © Jacqui Melville
Prop Styling: Nicole Herft
Colour Reproduction by p2d

Find this book on Cooked.
Cooked.com.au
Cooked.co.uk

Printed and bound in China by 1010
10 9 8 7 6 5 4 3 2 1